Imran Sohail
Sikandar Hayat

Network Security and DDoS

Imran Sohail
Sikandar Hayat

Network Security and DDoS

Cooperative Defense against DDoS attack Using GOSSIP protocol

LAP LAMBERT Academic Publishing

Impressum/Imprint (nur für Deutschland/ only for Germany)
Bibliografische Information der Deutschen Nationalbibliothek: Die Deutsche Nationalbibliothek verzeichnet diese Publikation in der Deutschen Nationalbibliografie; detaillierte bibliografische Daten sind im Internet über http://dnb.d-nb.de abrufbar.
Alle in diesem Buch genannten Marken und Produktnamen unterliegen warenzeichen-, marken- oder patentrechtlichem Schutz bzw. sind Warenzeichen oder eingetragene Warenzeichen der jeweiligen Inhaber. Die Wiedergabe von Marken, Produktnamen, Gebrauchsnamen, Handelsnamen, Warenbezeichnungen u.s.w. in diesem Werk berechtigt auch ohne besondere Kennzeichnung nicht zu der Annahme, dass solche Namen im Sinne der Warenzeichen- und Markenschutzgesetzgebung als frei zu betrachten wären und daher von jedermann benutzt werden dürften.

Coverbild: www.ingimage.com

Verlag: LAP LAMBERT Academic Publishing AG & Co. KG
Dudweiler Landstr. 99, 66123 Saarbrücken, Deutschland
Telefon +49 681 3720-310, Telefax +49 681 3720-3109
Email: info@lap-publishing.com

Herstellung in Deutschland:
Schaltungsdienst Lange o.H.G., Berlin
Books on Demand GmbH, Norderstedt
Reha GmbH, Saarbrücken
Amazon Distribution GmbH, Leipzig
ISBN: 978-3-8383-7009-5

Imprint (only for USA, GB)
Bibliographic information published by the Deutsche Nationalbibliothek: The Deutsche Nationalbibliothek lists this publication in the Deutsche Nationalbibliografie; detailed bibliographic data are available in the Internet at http://dnb.d-nb.de.
Any brand names and product names mentioned in this book are subject to trademark, brand or patent protection and are trademarks or registered trademarks of their respective holders. The use of brand names, product names, common names, trade names, product descriptions etc. even without a particular marking in this works is in no way to be construed to mean that such names may be regarded as unrestricted in respect of trademark and brand protection legislation and could thus be used by anyone.

Cover image: www.ingimage.com

Publisher: LAP LAMBERT Academic Publishing AG & Co. KG
Dudweiler Landstr. 99, 66123 Saarbrücken, Germany
Phone +49 681 3720-310, Fax +49 681 3720-3109
Email: info@lap-publishing.com

Printed in the U.S.A.
Printed in the U.K. by (see last page)
ISBN: 978-3-8383-7009-5

ACKNOWLEDGEMENT

First of all I would like to thank Almighty Allah who empowered me to finish this work with patience and dedication. I am very thankful to our supervisors **Charlott Eliasson** and **M. Hassan Islam** for their advice, guidance and support throughout our thesis. Their experience and vision enables us to polish our raw ideas.

I would like to thank my thesis partner Sikandar Hayat, whose dedication and cooperation helped me to achieve this milestone.

I am very thankful to my parents, brother, sister and especially my beloved wife for their support during the completion of my professional goal. I would also like to thank my friends M. Imran Shafi and Atiq ur Rehman for their moral support during my thesis work.

Imran Sohail

Apart from the completion of masters in telecommunication, I learn two things during my thesis work, co-operation and encouragement; cooperation was not only between me and Imran, but also between us and our supervisors, **Charlott Eliasson** and **M. Hassan Islam**. At the end, our hearts are full of encouragement, and this is not only from our supervisors but **Markus Fiedler** adds his positive and solid part too.

Sikandar Hayat

DEDICATION

We dedicate our thesis work to our beloved parents

Table of Contents

1. INTRODUCTION

1.1 Overview

DDoS attack is the greatest threat to network security in these days, in time detection of this attack is the main problem of DDoS attack, many other techniques and formulation has already been introduced to detect DDoS, but the problem still lies there. A smart attacker can penetrate the network by launching a DDoS attack as it doesn't have some common characteristics that can be classified as an attack. Currently available detection systems like IDS can be beaten easily by such attackers.

Keeping this in mind, we have proposed a distributed approach to detect DDoS attack at intermediate network with some more efficient and accurate manner. We make use of Gossip based scheme to multicast the information amongst the connected nodes with in the network. If any of the connected node reports an abnormal behavior in the packet, this node will share this anomaly with all the nodes and in the end a decision is calculated to declare the packet as friendly or attack and secure the whole network from DDoS attack.

1.2 (a) what is DoS Attack

A Denial of Service (DoS) is an attack with the purpose of thwart legitimate users from using a particular resource of network such as a website, web service, or computer system. If we look at the facts below, we can see just how much consumption of bandwidth can be in a simple enough attack.

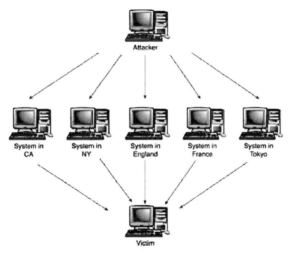

Figure 1.1 DoS attack

A single attack consists of Magnitude of 25.000 bytes/sec or 24 KB/sec. or 192 Kbps. if we Assume N as number of attackers and N=100 attackers = 192×100 = 18.7 Mbps DoS attack

If we multiply these facts exponentially by the number of attackers, one can launch such an extensive attack with great impact. [1]

1.2(b) What is DDoS Attack

A Distributed Denial of Service (DDoS) is a co-operational attack on the availability of services of a given target system or network that is indirectly launched through many compromised computing systems. The service or system which is directly under attack are called "primary victim" while the cooperated systems used to commence the attack are called the "secondary victims or zombies".

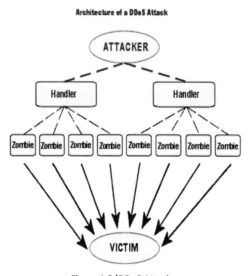

Figure 1.2 (DDoS Attack
Architecture)

The use of Secondary Victims in a DDoS attack provides the attacker with the ability to launch a larger and more disruptive attack while remaining unidentified, since the secondary victims actually perform the attack making it more difficult for network forensics to track down the real attacker [6, 10].

3

A Distributed Denial of Service (DDoS) attack is a global, coordinated attack on the availability of system's service or network resource. The DDoS attack instigates by sending a huge number of packets to the target machine through the real-time cooperation of a large number of hosts that are distributed over the Internet. The attack traffic consumes the bandwidth resources of the network or the computing resource at the target host, so that genuine and legal requests will be discarded. The effect of these attacks can vary from trivial hassle to the users of a web site, to severe financial sufferings to companies, dependent on their on-line availability to do business **[4, 6]**. DDoS attack has become an increasing threat to the network and Internet because of the easy availability of ready to use attack tools, which help to coordinate and execute a large-scale DDoS attack. Even an unsophisticated entity can launch a destructive attack using these tools. Available tools like TRINOO, TFN, TFN2K, and Stacheldraht have been used in DDoS attacks against renowned viable web sites, such as Amazon, and **EBay [11]** and even official websites like "Georgian and Lithuanian official websites". **[2, 3]**

A key problem when relating DDoS attacks is to detect them. There are several approaches that have been proposed for their detection. Most of them can be classified as either signature based or abnormal behavior based mechanism. As DDoS has no common signatures of attack, thus a sophisticated or experienced attacker may change the attack pattern frequently. However, DDoS traffic generated by today's tools often has characteristics that make it possible to distinguish it from normal traffic using statistical measurement **[5, 13, 12]**.

This abnormal behavior can be used to define methods to improve the detection accuracy at each individual node. Generally detection of this peculiar behavior of attack is easy near the victim. Nevertheless, this detection of the DDoS attack is too late at the victim network. The ideal location of DDoS attack detection is to stop as near to the source as possible, saving network resources and preventing clogging. However, DDoS attack does not have such characteristics which may help to detect and stop it near the source. To balance this tradeoff, detection of the DDoS attacks might be possible in the intermediate network. As the traffic is not amassed enough in the intermediate network, existing deployment detection systems is unable to detect DDoS attacks with high accuracy. To improve the detection accuracy, we need a standard shift instead of building revealing systems that operate in segregation, the need of time is to build a disseminated framework of detection nodes where heterogeneous systems can plug in and cooperate to achieve a better overall detection, which can monitor traffic and cooperate with other nodes. Conventional **Intrusion Detection Systems (IDS)** effect in a high false alarms when detect DDoS attacks. By cooperation, we can improve the accuracy of DDoS detection. However, a known network of large number of nodes in the Internet, we need a scalable and proficient well-organized architecture to split the information among the individual detection systems. The primary contribution of our report is to propose a global detection infrastructure by constructing an **overlay network** over the Internet. This infrastructure can provide dependable, trustworthy, rapid and extensive cooperation among individual detection nodes for the sake of improvement in the accuracy of DDoS attack detection in the intermediate network.

Given the large scale of the Internet and crucial purpose of this infrastructure, we need consistent and reliable communication mechanism to exchange the attack information.

1.3 Differences Between DoS And DDoS Attack

DoS Attack	DDoS Attack
A Denial of Service (DoS) attack is an attack which is launched against a system component to prevent the legitimate traffic from the specified network resources such as a website, web service, or computer system.	A **Distributed Denial of Service (DDoS) attack** is a coordinated attack on the availability of services of a given target system or network that is launched indirectly through many compromised computing systems.
DoS attacks are unable to attack large bandwidth websites. One upstream client cannot generate enough bandwidth to cripple major megabit websites.	**DDoS attacks** can attack larger bandwidth websites. Because (DDoS) attack uses many computers (called ZOMBIES) to launch a coordinated DoS attack against one or more targets.
DoS attacks are usually unresponsive to traffic control.	**DDoS** attacks are responsive to traffic control
Dos attack packets are MALACIOUS	**DDoS** attack packets are not

6

i.e. (deliberately harmful).	malicious in nature they are like genuine packets.
DoS attacks are unpredictable.	**DDoS** attacks are predictable.
DoS attacks are also called Bandwidth attack. Because it consumes the critical resources in the network service.	**DDoS** attacks are also called Flash crowd attacks, because it occurs as a large number of legitimate users access a server at the same time.
In **DoS** attacks network became congested.	In **DDoS** attacks network become congested.
In **DoS** attack server became overloaded.	In **DDoS** attack server became overloaded too.
In **DoS** attack traffic type may be any.	In **DDoS** attack traffic type is mostly web traffic.
In **DoS** attack attacker cannot be offline during the attack.	In **DDoS** attack the attacker can be offline when the attack occurs.
DoS attack depends upon system or protocol weaknesses.	**DDoS** attacks do not depend upon system or protocol weaknesses.
DoS attacks are old type of attacks and can be detected.	**DDoS** attacks are new type of attacks and hard to detect.
DoS attack over the internet can be target at a user, a host computer or a	But **DDoS attacks** can attack lager websites and DNS servers as well.

network.	

Table 1.1 (Difference between DoS & DDoS)

A simple analogy might clarify the difference between **DoS** and a **DDoS**, and point out some interesting subtleties. If a bored teen-ager repeatedly 'prank' calls your telephone, you may soon get tired of answering, and may start to ignore subsequent incoming calls. The teenager has successfully performed a **DoS** attack on your telephone service, because you are denied normal telephone services (even though you denied them yourself, by choosing not to answer). However, it is easy to screen incoming calls from the teen-agers number, so in many cases, not all services are interrupted -- just incoming calls from a specific number. This also make the location of the attacker easy to trace, and therefore relatively easy to stop.

If, however, the teen-ager called a local radio station and duped them into believing that you had special concert tickets for sale at a very low price, causing your telephone number to be broadcast, you may be inundated with many 100's of calls, from many people. In this **DDoS** example, you are again denied normal phone services (the **DoS** component) but the distributed nature of the attack means that most calls that do not originate from a known number would need to be blocked, and if enough people responded, almost no calls could get through. In this case, questioning or tracing any of the apparent attackers is pointless, since they have been duped into calling, and have no evidence to offer at all about the identity of the real attacker. In fact, only the original point of attack (in this case, a call

8

to the radio station) is of any interest in determining who attacked. The teenager may not have even phoned you (so the real attacker, the initiator of the **DDoS**, did not participate in the actual **DoS** attack).**[17].**

1.4DDoS Background

Later in the month July 2008, during Russian- Georgia conflict, a major cyber attack was launched on Georgian state computer servers and they were hijacked for more than 24 hours. Even the Georgian president's official web site was already under DDoS attack, Following is a list provided by the Georgian officials that shows the servers or ISP's which were being used as compromised hosts or zombies during the DDoS attack.[2]

```
ping: president.gov.ge
```

location	result	min. rtt	avg. rtt	max. rtt
Florida, U.S.A.	Okay	50.7	51.6	52.2
New York, U.S.A.	Okay	29.5	30.6	31.6
Stockholm, Sweden	Okay	123.3	125.4	130.3
Copenhagen, Denmark	Okay	109.4	109.8	110.6
Austin1, U.S.A.	Okay	56.9	60.5	63.8
Amsterdam2, Netherlands	Okay	107.0	109.2	128.6
Paris, France	Okay	102.1	102.3	102.4
Madrid, Spain	Okay	126.7	129.3	147.4
Amsterdam, Netherlands	Okay	98.1	105.4	140.3
Munchen, Germany	Okay	117.5	118.3	120.0
Hong Kong, China	Okay	254.0	256.8	279.4
Vancouver, Canada	Okay	79.3	84.9	132.9
Zurich, Switzerland	Okay	119.5	126.4	178.7
Austin, U.S.A.	Packets lost (100%)			
Santa Clara, U.S.A.	Packets lost (100%)			
Chicago, U.S.A.	Packets lost (100%)			
Shanghai, China	Okay	265.9	266.2	266.6
Sydney, Australia	Packets lost (100%)			
Melbourne, Australia	Packets lost (100%)			
Singapore, Singapore	Packets lost (100%)			
Johannesburg, South Africa	Packets lost (100%)			
London, United Kingdom	Packets lost (100%)			
Lille, France	Packets lost (100%)			
Amsterdam3, Netherlands	Packets lost (100%)			
Cologne, Germany	Packets lost (100%)			
San Francisco, U.S.A.	Packets lost (100%)			
Cagliari, Italy	Packets lost (100%)			
Krakow, Poland	Packets lost (100%)			
Mumbai, India	Packets lost (100%)			
Porto Alegre, Brazil	Packets lost (100%)			

Fig 1.3 (Attack report)

During Russia and Lithuania cyber war, more than 300 private and government site of Lithuania were hacked by some unidentified hackers later in August, the hackers pasted Soviet symbols, the hammer and sickle and also the five pointed star. It was investigated that the hackers used the Zombies (compromised systems) located in France and Sweden to use them for these attacks, interestingly these victim sites were also hosted by the same ISP's. **[3].**

1.5 DDoS Attack Classification

There are two main classes of DDoS attacks: **bandwidth depletion** and **resource depletion** attacks.

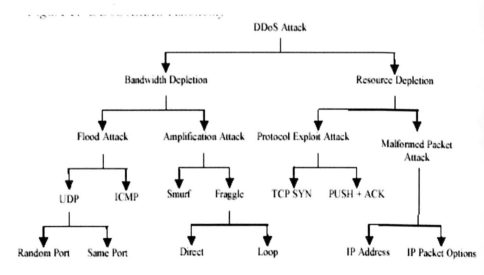

Figure 1.4 (Attack Classification)

1.5.1 A bandwidth Depletion Attack

This attack is designed to flood the victim network with unwanted traffic that prevents legitimate or lawful traffic from reaching the victim system.

Bandwidth depletion attacks can be characterized as

- Flood attacks
- Amplification attacks.

1.5.1.1 Flood Attacks

Flooded based attack (DDoS attack) launches by sending a huge volume of traffic to a target machine with the help of zombies clog the network bandwidth of target machine with IP traffic. This process decelerate system's performance, causes system crash by flooding network bandwidth and thwart the legitimate users to access the system. **ICMP (Internet Control Message Protocol) packets and UDP (User Datagram Protocol) packets both are used to launch flood attacks.** Specific or random ports of the target machine are attacked by the huge volume of UDP packets in **UDP flood attack**. This confuses the victim system to process the incoming data and by finding out the applications requesting this process or data. If no application is running on targeted port of victim system, an ICMP packet indicating "destination port unreachable" message will be sent out by victim machine **[15]**. It happens a lot, the IP addresses of attacking packets are spoofed by the tool used to launch DDoS attack in order to conceal the identity of the zombies so that returned packets never goes to the secondary victim (Zombies) but to the spoofed IP addresses. The network bandwidth of connections around the victim system may also be get filled due to the UDP flood attack. Systems which are located near

12

the victim may also be affected by this attack. **ICMP flood attack** is launched by sending a huge volume of "Ping" **ICMP ECHO REPLY** packets to the victim by the zombies. The network bandwidth of target machine flooded with a combination of request and respond traffic and a spoofed IP address of ICMP packet may be used during this attack. **[14]**

1.5.1.2 Amplification Attacks

An attacker or zombies are included in an amplification attack by sending messages to an already broadcast IP address; a reply from the victim system is enforced to send by all those subnets under this broadcast address. Most of routers have broadcast IP address features. If the destination address is set with the broadcast IP address from a sender, usually the router keeps an image (Replication) of the packet and throws it to all the IP addresses which are in the range of that broadcast IP address. Under this attack to amplify and to get the reflection or respond of attack traffic this broadcast IP address is used. This amplification and attack traffic reflection reduces the bandwidth of victim system. A direct broadcast message or agents can be used to increase the number of packets or the volume of attacking traffic. This attack facilitates an attacker to use the machines as zombies surrounded by the broadcast network to send the direct broadcast message without requiring the access to the systems or without installing and using agent software.

DDoS **Smurf attack** can be the example of amplification attack. Masquerade packets consisting victim's IP address as its return address are sent to the system which supports broadcast addressing simply know as network amplifier. ICMP ECHO REQUESTs (Ping) packets are typical

13

attacking packet for such attack that demands the receiving system to reply back in form of ICMP ECHO REPLY packet. All the systems in this broadcast network extension receive this ICMP ECHO REQUEST by the amplifier and reply back to the requesting system's IP address i.e. the victim's IP address **[8]**. This amplification can be 10 to 100 times of original packet.

[7, 9]

DDoS **Fraggle Attack** is another example, UDP Echo packets are used for amplification instead of ICMP ECHO REPLY, but the purpose and pattern is same as DDoS Smurf Attack. A small difference in Fraggle attack is, **UDP ECHO** packets are sent on the port which supports character generation (in UNIX port 19, chargen), and these UDP packets are spoofed as return address with the victim's echo service (in Unix Port 7, echo), this cause an infinite loop. Character Generation is the main target of UDP Fraggle attack packet to the systems within the broadcast address range. As a respond of each character an echo service will be sent to the victim system, and character generator (spoofed with victim's echo service) will receive echo packet, and this process will be repeated. Fraggle attack can damage more than Smurf attack by generating more bad traffic.

1.5.2 A Resource Depletion Attack

A resource depletion attack is to bind the resources of the target system (Victim). The main target of this attack type is the server or the process of the target machine, and to unable the system to legalize the request for a service.

Characteristics of Resource Depletion

- Protocol Exploit attack
- Malformed Packet attack

1.5.2.1 Protocol Exploit Attacks

Two basic mishandlings of **Protocol Exploit Attack** are the misuse of **TCP-SYN** and **PUSH-ACK** protocol. In TCP-SYN attack the attacker gives instructions to Zombie to send forged **TCP-SYN** requests to the target machine or server, these fake requests bind the processor's resources of the server (Target Machine) and paralyze the server not to respond for legal requests. The main purpose to launch this attack is to exploit the three-way handshake built in between the sender and the receiver by sending a huge number of **TCP-SYN** packet to the target machine with spoofed or fake IP addresses, which causes the system to respond to an unknown requesting system with ACK-SYN packets. When the Server (Target Machine) processes the huge volume of SYN requests and there is no response of ACK-SYN requests, the server runs out of the resources of processor and memory and eventually server becomes unable to respond to the legitimate users.

The 2nd part of Resource Depletion attack is **PUSH-ACK** attack. In this attack, the attacker sends TCP packets by setting **PUSH** and **ACK** bits to 1. The triggering of **PUSH-ACK** bits in TCP header enforce the target machine (Victim) to drop off all data in the buffer (TCP buffer, weather it is full or not) and send an ACK when the task is completed. The receiving system will not be able to process the huge numbers of incoming packets if

15

the process is repeated with multiple agents and eventually the target machine will crash. **[16]**

1.5.2.2 Malformed Packet Attacks

In this type of attack, Zombies are instructed by the attacker to send IP packets which are formed incorrectly to the target machine with the intention to crash it. We can divide Malformed Packet into two types. **IP address attack** and **IP packet options attack**.

In **IP address attack**, the IP packet is reformed by changing the source and destination with same IP address. This reformation of packet confuses the target system and causes a system crash. On the other hand, in the 2nd type of attack **IP Packet Options attack** the IP packet is altered by setting all QoS (Quality of Service) bits to 1 and by randomizing the optional fields. This alteration causes the target machine to use additional time of processing to analyze the traffic. In order to exhaust the processing of victim machine, this process is multiplied and causes a system crash.

1.6 DDoS Characteristics

The reasons of unsuccessful detection and protection of DDoS attacks can be due to the following features.

- To overwhelm the victim, DDoS attack generates a huge volume of flow. The victim is unable to defend itself even it detects the attack, because the detection is too late to be guarded. This is why the revealing and the protection of DDoS attack must be closer to the source or somewhere in the network.

16

- The legitimate packets and attack packets are hard to differentiate as both can be identical to each other. For a successful attack the attacker is sending a huge volume of data regardless what the data contents are. Moreover, from an individual system, the volume of data packets can be very low to be detected by the local administrators. So based on single site, the rates of detection system will be either high positive or high negative.

- Mostly spoofed IP source address is being used in DDoS attacks to masquerade the agent machines. This can also be used to commit the reflector attacks. The DDoS attacks are so large in the scale that it is nearly impossible to trace the agent machine.

- Due to the identical characteristics of traffic which is generated by the tools available today, statistical analysis based detection is possible. But DDoS attack detection still has flaws due to the internet's busty nature.

1.7 DDoS Attack Can Be Done In Two Ways

1.7.1 Direct Attack

To block the incoming link to a victim, often the victim responds it with Reset Packet.

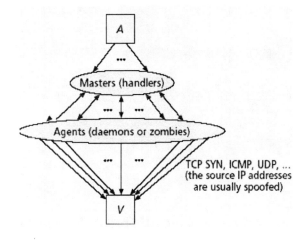

Figure 1.5 (Direct Attack)

1.7.2 Reflector Attack

A response required packet whose source address is set to the victim's address is sent to the reflector by the attacker. A response packet of attack packet type is returned to the victim.

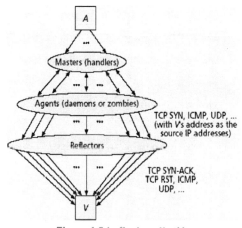

Figure 1.6 (reflector attack)

2. GOSSIP PROTOCOL

2.1 Gossip Protocol

Figure 2.1(gossip protocol)

Gossiping is an efficient way of distributing information in vigorous systems. Many simulations have been used to design or evaluate the gossiping algorithms. In spite of this, these algorithms seldom manage numerous real-world problems, which are mostly unseen or unnoticed in the simulations. e.g. node failures, message or packet loss, information exchange and firewalls. The primary unit of Gossip architecture is the Gossip node.

2.2 Gossip Node

Some characteristics of gossip node are listed below.

- Email sender information is stored.
- Information about other gossip nodes is stored.
- Tweaks this information according to direct occurrences and feedback.
- Status score is provided when an identity is supplied.
- When and identity submit feedback on messages it accepts and stores this feedback.

2.3 Confidence Value

The measurement of confidence rating is said to be, the reputation score a GOSSIP node reports for an identity.

Following function can be used to measure the confidence rating of a GOSSIP node.

Confidence($R(i)$) = [sum(o) / N] * age

Where

R is the reputation score

i the given identity for which reputation score is reported.

N is the reputation cache size.

And age can be calculated as

age = [age(0)/age(n)]*100

age(n) is the duration of computation in seconds.

Age(o) is the duration of locally last transaction with the identity (measured in seconds).

This shows that confidence value provides the age of data (How old this data is) and the reflected amount of data which a node has for a particular identity.

2.3.1 How Reputation Is Computed

To compute the reputation one of the two following conditions must be fulfilled.

1. When a query of TTL = 0 is received on GOSSIP node.

2. None or more GOSSIP nodes timed out while a node is waiting for their query response and at the same time the remaining nodes supply the query response.

For this computation the GOSSIP node verifies UMIS (Unique Message Identification String) which it has recently seen. If UMIS in the query does not match with the node's recently seen UMIS, it starts computing reputation score and confidence rate for that particular identity. After computing the reputation and the confidence value, this data will be sent to the source of query.

2.3.2 Gossip Node Accepts Three Forms Of Input

- Acceptance of query from a Peer or MTA.

- Accepts response from peer or MTA

- Accepts feedback from a mechanism

2.3.3 Structure Of A Gossip Query

Four parts of a GOSSIP query

- Identification of input as query through a tag

- Identity of Query.

- A TTL value (Time-to-Live)

- A unique string called UMIS (Unique Message Identification String)

2.4 Time To Live (TTL)

A query TTL restrains the depth of a query which will be broadcast in GOSSIP network. At the time of deployment TTL is set according to the value given by administrator when the mail server instigates the query. TTL reduced as the query spreads through the network and this dissemination will stop when TTL reaches zero.

2.5 Unique Message-Identification String (UMIS)

Unique Message Identification String in short known as UMIS is created by the GOSSIP MTA agent. This UMIS is placed as GOSSIP-ID in the incoming message.

2.6 How Queries Are Received

A prearranged TCP port is set to receive the incoming query on a GOSSIP node. Source IP is compared to MTAs and Peers by the GOSSIP node when the connection is established. If a match is found in the list of addresses the connection will get permission for proceeding else the connection will be reset. SSL may or may not be used to encrypt this connection between MTA and GOSSIP node but the connection between peers is always encrypted using SSL.

2.6.1 Query Processing

Upon the establishment of query connection, the next step done by GOSSIP node is to accept and parse the query and waits for the response from the receiver. TTL value is calculated to make the further decision, a reputation information and confidence value are calculated and responded if TTL is observed as zero other wise TTL is decreased by 1 unless it reaches null. This calculation is passed to each of the peers which will either send responses to GOSSIP node or a time out occurs. GOSSIP node calculates the reputation and confidence value on the satisfaction of any one of the condition, either null value of TTL or time out occurrence and sends this information to the original sender. An acknowledgement is sent by the sender and the TCP connection is closed or this connection may be aborted if the response is received before the occurrence of time out.

2.6.2 Confidence Value

The measurement of confidence rating is said to be, the reputation score a GOSSIP node reports for an identity.

Following function can be used to measure the confidence rating of a GOSSIP node.

$Confidence(R(i)) = [sum(o) / N] * age$

Where

R is the reputation score

i the given identity for which reputation score is reported.

N is the reputation cache size.

And age can be calculated as

age = [age(0)/age(n)]*100

age(n) is the duration of computation in seconds.

Age(o) is the duration of locally last transaction with the identity (measured in seconds).

This shows that confidence value provides the age of data (How old this data is) and the reflected amount of data which a node has for a particular identity.

2.6.3 How Reputation Is Computed

To compute the reputation one of the two following conditions must be fulfilled.

1. When a query of TTL = 0 is received on GOSSIP node.

2. None or more GOSSIP nodes timed out while a node is waiting for their query response and at the same time the remaining nodes supply the query response.

For this computation the GOSSIP node verifies UMIS (Unique Message Identification String) which it has recently seen. If UMIS in the query does not match with the node's recently seen UMIS, it starts computing reputation score and confidence rate for that particular identity. After computing the reputation and the confidence value, this data will be sent to the source of query.

2.7 Attack Information Sharing

Anomaly detection model mainly requires the low false positive rates and high positive rates.

- Low positive rates in %: Normalcy variations.
- High positive rates in %: Anomalies Detected.

System performance can be affected by two major factors. Namely the cost of the mechanism used for information sharing, and how long it takes to make decision? (Delay in decision making). If multicast or broadcast is used to distribute information, a huge number of messages are publicized (transmit) gratuitously, as all routers are not in the path of the attack destination. A heavy load on network is a major cause due to DDoS attack, this major cause of overloading network restricts us to use multicasting or broadcasting for local detection information sharing as it will further slows down the network. Another inadequate resource to share information during DDoS attack is communication bandwidth. For that reason the information sharing regarding attack should contains of only small messages. Another way which may create bottlenecks is the use of protocol, collecting local data at a single node and it may cause message implosion at the node.

To overcome these problems and reduce control message overhead, gossip based protocols have been developed and introduced, these gossip based protocols own high consistency and scalability of message delivery,

One difference between gossip protocols and commonly used multicast protocol is, gossip protocols do not require much synchronization as other do. In gossip based protocols, every node contacts other node(s) (Randomly chosen) and exchange information with each other. This widespread of information resembles with spread of plague, and control fault tolerance. Protocol based on gossip often does not need any mechanism for recovery while experiencing restrained overhead compared to best deterministic protocols. The algorithm below shows the structure of gossip protocol running at each node n.

when (node n builds a new pair (conf, dest)) {

While (node n believes that not enough of its neighbors have received (const, dest) pair){

m = a neighbor node of p;

send(conf, dest) pair to m;

}

}

If we compare gossip protocol with traditional multicast or broadcast protocols, gossip protocol has a smaller operating cost but longer time is required to get the message at each node. If we are looking at the reduced distributed cost we also need the rapid information delivery as multicast or broadcast protocols. Another alternate is directional gossip [20], which is mainly intended to reduce the communication cost or overhead of conventional gossip protocol. In our line of tactic, we used a customized

26

directional gossip approach. Our assumption is that each distinct node knows its direct neighbors in the network. We can describe our gossiping protocol as follows: A distinct node sends a pair of (conf, dest) with probability 1 to a node which comes in the path to destination node. The receiving node spreads this pair of (conf, dest) to all the nodes in network randomly. At time t, each node i keeps a list of (confk, destk) pairs. We use a different algorithm to share and spread DDoS attacks information, this algorithm is described as follows.

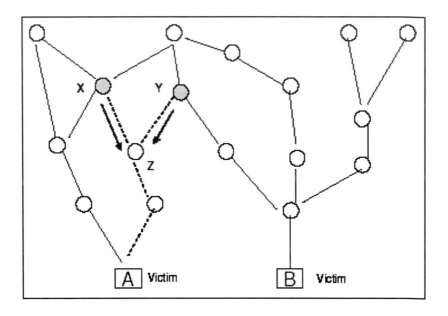

Figure 1-13 (Gossip strategy in our approach)

27

2.8 Feedback Mechanism

A prearranged TCP port is set to receive feedback for a GOSSIP node. This feedback consists of two items.

- UMIS which is related or coupled with a particular message.
- Integer value (0, 1) is used to evaluate the message as spam or harm.

After accepting the information from feedback mechanism GOSSIP node abort the connection. Then UMIS will be put side by side with a First In First Out (FIFO) cache with a size of P. this size P is from the previously seen UMIS strings. If UMIS is already in the cache, it is detached from the cache and the new costing or assessment is attached with the ID's data.

3. PROPOSED TECHNIQUE

After studying all the previous approaches like **Covariance Analysis Approach**, **Source Router Approach, Integrated Approach** and **Statistical approach**. We have made our new approach called **Cooperative Defense against DDoS Attacks**: -

3.1 Cooperative Defense Against DDos Attacks

DDoS attacks can be detected by analyzing affected or degraded services as DDoS attacks are transmitted across the internet and directed towards the victim, but to launch a defense measurement against a DDoS attack near the victim is not a smart idea because the resources are already under heavy load and the victim can not properly respond to attacks. Therefore it is recommended to stop the attacks near the attack sources which are also helpful to save network resources and can reduce the congestion. However, DDoS attacks can't be fully detected and filtered near the source.

The question is now, what is the ideal place to deploy the defense system against DDoS attack? A best solution for this is at the intermediate network. At this middle part of the propagation stream, we assume that DDoS attacks create more aggregation than the normal flow and consume more bandwidth as the attacks come more and more close to victim. However this congestion causes less congestion, making it hard to detect the attacks in single domain, therefore introducing shared information over several domains makes it possible to detect the DDoS attacks earlier.

There are two main stages in the proposed detection scheme. During first stage, each local node identifies the traffic anomalies using profile of normal traffic which is constructed using stream sampling algorithm. Given the dynamic nature of the Internet, the conclusions are based on this mechanism is just a lot of false positives. The next phase, we can improve the accuracy of detection of media by using gossip based multicast based on sharing information among different nodes. To improve the safety and reliability, our system is based on an overlay network which consists of local nodes such as routers with a DDoS attack detection and packet filtering function. An overlay network is a virtual network using the existing network. It consists of routers, and tunnels. Tunnels are paths in a database of network information and links on the top line. Each of the components, that are routers, can participate in more than one overlay at a time, or one of the coverage in several ways. As a result, it is a natural form of the network and can be an overlay network link. Multiple links can increase the flexibility of the network, and the more flexible the network is probably less vulnerable to attack.

Moreover, by building a comprehensive, self-organization and resilience overlay networks over the Internet, peer nodes in an overlay network can provide information about the attack in a fast and reliable way. Individual nodes are discovered at the exit routers and work as a separate system to collect all relevant information and identifying local DDoS attacks. The system then uses the overlay network to share information obtained from the detection by the use of gossip protocols based on epidemic algorithms over the Internet.

This can be illustrated in the Figure

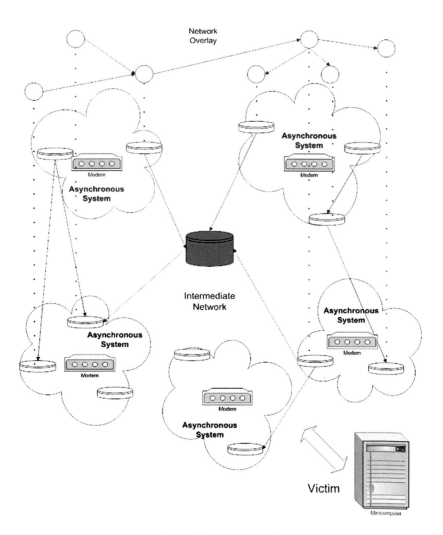

Figure 3-1(overlay network)

Internal node detection can be very complicated, but can be divided into six conceptual pieces. Determining the internal node can be very complicated, but the concept can be done by dividing it into six units. Measuring the movement of local traffic is achieved by traffic measurement module. Further, this local identification mechanism uses this information to identify the local anomalies. On the same way, the information about the anomalies of the neighboring nodes is gathered and will be sent to the cooperative anomaly detection module, which makes use of global message diffusion module. Finally, the response units of any local module are informed about the actions to be taken to protect against the attacks.

3.2 Attack Detection Procedure

In our opinion, aggress routers are key elements necessary to identify the attack, and to provide the necessary information to respond these attacks, therefore these key routers have to coordinate with each other to carry out this task. This mechanism can improve the accuracy and speed of detection of DDoS attacks. The operations on these egress routers are described below:

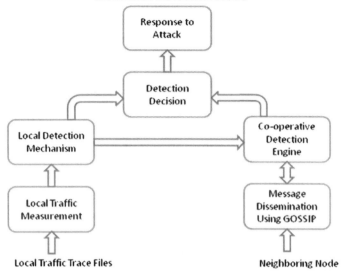

Figure 3.2 (individual detection node)

- On the detection of an abnormality, each local node shares this information to its neighboring through gossip. If every node reports similar information, DDoS attack detection is declared after sharing this information with all nodes over the network.
- This information is compared with the local timestamp and discards the expired message after evaluating them with time stamp.
- On the confirmation of a DDoS attack, an effective counter defense is deployed to prevent the consequences of the attack.

We can make a combination of our proposed approach with justifying or rate limit technologies to get rid of anomalies before their execution.

4. OUR IMPLEMENTATION

In this project we proposed a new technique to detect the DDoS attack using gossip protocol. As gossip is use for database management we use this database for DoS signatures. Every node has its own database of signatures. The end result is based on aggregate value proposed by different gossip nodes if the end value is positive then it is an attack packet else a friendly packet.

Our design consists of three types of packets.

- Topology Discovery Packet (TDP)

- Signature Message (Sig_Msg)

- Acknowledgement Signature Message (Ack_Sig_Msg)

4.1 Topology Discovery Packet (TDP)

This packet use to discover neighbours by simply broadcasting. Consist of following phases

- Packet Send

- Packet Received

4.1.1 Packet Send

The node broadcast this packet at its out gate by setting **source id** and **hops count** and leave other fields to be filled by the node that receive this packet, at this stage packet frame look like as follows.

Source_ID	Target _ID	Gate_ID	Hop_Count	Processing_Delay
Src_id			0	

Figure 4-1(TDP)

4.1.2 Packet Received

When packet is received by node it has to make decision based on **hop count** as follows:-

- Hop count equals 0

- Hop count equals 1

4.1.2.1 Hop count equals 0

When hop count is zero (0) the node who receive the packet know that it is the new node who join the network it simply fill the blank field of **target id** and **processing delay** by setting it with its own node id and time taken to process the packet (ideally zero in our case) respectively then broadcast the packet at out gates at this stage packet frame look like as follows.

Source_ID	Target _ID	Gate_ID	Hop_Count	Processing_Delay
src_id	my_id		1	Ideally zero

Figure 4-2(TDP)

4.1.2.2 Hop count equals 1

When hop count equals to one (1) the receiving node make decision on source id it has following conditions.

- Source Id Not Matches

- Source Id Matches

4.1.2.2.1 Source Id Not Matches

If the source id doesn't match to the receiving node id it just simply discards the packet.

4.1.2.2.2 Source Id Matches

If source matches to the receiving node id it filled the remaining field i.e. **gate id** the receiving gate from where the packet is arrived and hence the TDP frame look like.

Source_ID	Target _ID	Gate_ID	Hop_Count	Processing_Delay
src_id	my_id	rcv_gate_id	1	Ideally zero

Figure 4-3(TDP)

And the node just updates information about its neighboring node in its forwarding table.

4.1.3 Forwarding Table

Forwarding table is simply the table which maintains the list of neighbouring nodes. It consists of following essential fields.

- Source Id

- Target Id

- Gate Id

36

- Delay

Source Id, **Target Id** and **Gate Id** is taken from packet received by node and **Delay** is calculated by a formulae is given below.

Delay = (end_time - TDP_pack->timestamp() - TDP_pack-> getProcessing_delay()) / 2

end_time is the time when packet arrived at receiving node.

timestamp is the time when packet is send by the node.

getProcessing_delay is the time taken to process the packet.

After topology discovery every node maintains its own forwarding table. Forwarding table of some nodes are as follows.

Figure 4-4

4.1.4 Flow Diagram Of Topology Discovery Packet

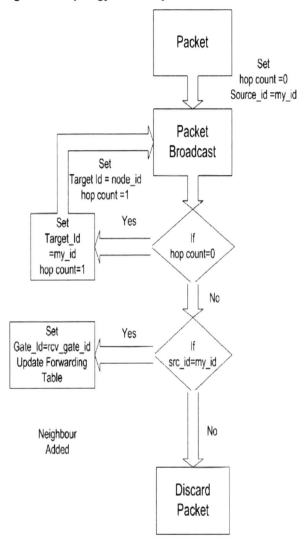

Figure 4.5 (TDP- Packet)

4.2 Signature Message (Sig_Msg)

This packet contains the message. In our design this packet is generated by **node 1.** We are considering node 1 as packet sniffer who gives us packet to be processed by our gossip network, and result is calculated at **node 2.**

4.2.1 Packet Generation

This is done by node 1 who creates the packet in our design we create two types of packet

- Attack

- Friendly

Attack packet contain attack signature in its payload and **friendly packet** contain signature other than attack signature. These packets are randomly generated by node1.

The packet has following fields.

- Sequence No.

- Node_id

- Delay

- Signature(Payload)

The signature packet on generation looks like as follows:

Sequence_No	Node_ID	Delay	DoS Signature
1	Scr_id	Depends upon the topology	attack / friendly

Figure 4-6(sig_msg)

4.2.2 Receiving Packet

On receiving Sig_Msg packet a node perform two major operations on packet as follows.

- Process Packet

- Forward Packet

4.2.2.1 Process Packet

In process packet the arrived packet is checked by node file which contain signatures of DDoS attack. If the packet payload contains the signature that matches the signature file of the node it sets the attack flag and send acknowledgement of the signature packet back from where the packet arrived.

4.2.2.2 Forward Packet

In forward packet the arrived packet is sent forward to neighboring node after processing by the node. Node sets the source id field with its own node id. The packet is forward on the basis of delay, the packet is sent first to the neighboring node which has lowest delay and at last which has highest delay value. Before forwarding packet the packet looks like as following.

Sequence_No	Node_ID	Delay	DoS Signature
1	My_id	Depends upon the topology	attack / friendly

Figure 4-7(forward packet)

4.2.3 Flow Diagram Of Signature Message (Sig_Msg)

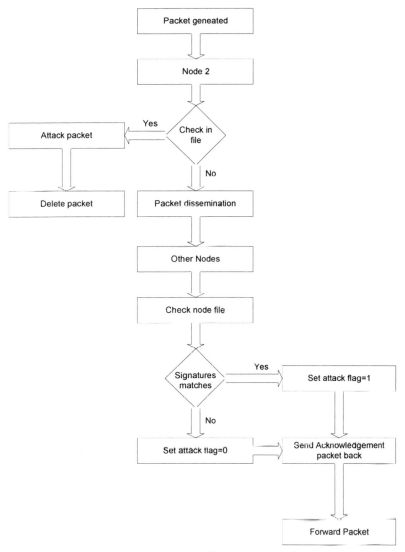

Figure 4-8 (SIG_Msg_Flowchart)

4.3 Acknowledgement Signature Message (Ack_Sig_Msg)

This packet contains the result of signature packet whether it is an attack or not. Every node sets attack flag after checking from its signature file and send acknowledgement back from where the packet arrived.

This packet contains the following fields.

- Sequence No.

- Attack flag

- Node id

Sequence no tells us sequence of packet for which the acknowledgement is arrived **attack flag** tells whether the packet with specific sequence no is attack or friendly and **node id** tells which node is declaring whether its an attack or not.

The packet of Ack_Sig_Msg looks like following.

Sequence_No	Node_ID	Attack_Flag
1	my_id	1 / 0

Figure 4-9(Ack_Sig_Msg)

4.4 Aggregation

The aggregation in our design is done by node 2.whenever a signature message arrives on node it checks the payload of the packet by its own signature file and set the attack flag if it is an attack packet and set zero if it is a friendly packet. On receiving Ack_sig_Msg the node checks its node id

43

it its node id is not 2 it passed the packet from where the Sig_Msg arrives. If the node id is 2 it checked the attack flag, if the flag is 1 it just increment the event value and if its not an attack then it decrement the event value.

4.5 Announcing Result

The result is announced when announce event occurred. It just count the event value if the value Is greater than negative one (-1) it declared that's an attack and updates the signature file of node 2 which is used whenever the same packet occurred it just discard from node 2 so that the design become efficient, and if the value is less than zero (0) it declared that's an friendly packet.

4.6 Flow diagram of Acknowledgement Signature Message Ack_Sig_Msg)

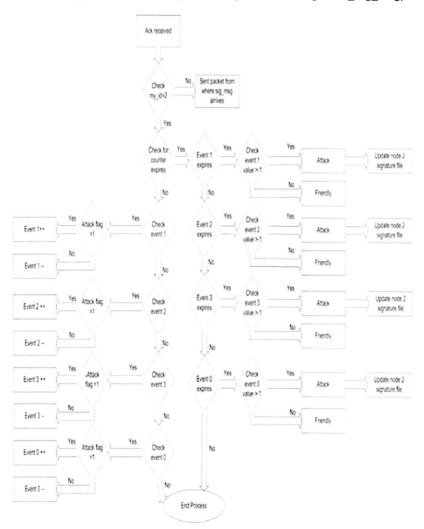

Figure 4-10

5. CONCLUSION AND FUTURE WORK

DDoS attack is the greatest threat to network security in these days, in time detection of this attack is the main problem of DDoS attack, many other techniques and formulation has already been introduced to detect DDoS, but the problem still lies there. The introduced techniques can detect the attack but may be the time it is too late for the prevention. Our proposed mechanism is a distributed mechanism to detect DDoS attack that monitors the network traffic continuously. The basic reason of effectiveness of our proposed design is the multicasting packet. This multicasting packet is based on the delay; this delay will be in ascending order. Each node in the network analyzes the packet and informs the neighboring nodes whether the packet is an attack packet or friendly packet. This information is sent to the query node from all nodes where the result is calculated. We simulate our proposed mechanism of defense against DDoS attack using omnet++ version 4.0. In our simulation node 2 is responsible for the filtration of traffic. In the simulation, node 2 kept the information of filtered traffic and updated its signature file with attack packets information. Using that information in signature file it discarded the attack packets and release the friendly packet if found. Seeing the results and output of our simulation we can conclude that the simulation was working as per our expectation.

Future work will be dependent on the information and susceptibility gathered from scanning more topologies. The utilization of intelligent GOSSIP strategy is more effective when a GOSSIP node gets as much topology information as possible. This GOSSIP strategy may include the reduction of information sharing overhead. If we equip our strategy with such highly developed and glassy information our approach can work more efficiently. During our work we explored some questions; those questions are still needed to be tackled. Optimal gossip period is one of the main questions along with some algorithm questions. This approach can be tested on a real network with real attack packets.

REFERENCES

[1] Andrew Noyes National Journal's Technology Daily April 5, 2007 DDoS attacks

[2] Coordinated Russia vs Georgia cyber attack in progress
http://blogs.zdnet.com/security/?p=1670&tag=rbxccnbzd1 (July 2008)

[3] 300 Lithuanian sites hacked by Russian hackers
http://blogs.zdnet.com/security/?p=1408&tag=rbxccnbzd1 (August 2008)

[4] Rocky K. C. Chang, "Defending Against Flooding-Based, Distributed Denial-of-Service Attacks: A Tutorial," IEEE Communications Magazine (A Special Issue on Telecommunication Network Security), vol. 40, no. 10,pp. 42-51, 2002.

[5] H. Wang, D. Zhang, and K. G. Shin, "Detecting SYN flooding attacks," In Proceeding of IEEE Infocom'2002,June 2002.

[6] D. G. Andersen, H. Balakrishnan, M. Frans Kaashoek and R. Morris, "Resilient Overlay Networks" in the Proceedings of 18th ACM SOSP 2001, Banff, Canada, October 2001.

[7] T. M. Gil and M. Poleto, "MULTOPS: a data-structure for banndwidth attack detection", In proceedings of 10th Usenix Security Symposium, August 2001.

[8] Salim Hariri, Tushneem Dharmagadda, Modukuri Ramkishore, Guangzhi Qu, C.S Raghavendra,"Vulnerability Analysis of Faults/Attacks in Network Centric Systems", PDCS 2003

[9] J. Mirkovic, G. Prier and P. Reiher, "Attacking DDoS at the Source", Proceedings of ICNP 2002, pp. 312-321, Paris, France, November 2002.

[10] T. Peng, C. Leckie and R. Kotagiri, "Protection from Distributed Denial of Service Attack Using History-based IP Filtering", IEEE International Conference on Communications (ICC 2003), Anchorage, Alaska, USA, May,2003.

[11] J. Mirkovic, M. Robinson, P. Reiher, and G.Kuenning, "Alliance Formation for DDoS Defense," Proceedings of the New Security Paradigms Workshop, ACM SIGSAC, August 2003.

[12] S. Zhang and P. Dasgupta, "Denying Denial of Service Attacks: A Router Based Solution," The 2003 International Conference on Internet Computing, June 2003.

[13] Aditya Akella, Ashwin Bharambe, Mike Reiter and Srinivasan Seshan, "Detecting DDoS Attacks on ISP Networks",ACM SIGMOD/PODS Workshop on Management and Processing of Data Streams (MPDS), FCRC2003, San Diego, CA.

[14] Jun Li, Peter Reiher, and Gerald Popek, "Resilient Self-Organizing Overlay Networks for Security Update delivery", IEEE Journal on Selected Areas in Communications, special issue on Service Overlay Networks, Vol. 22, No. 1, January 2004.
[15] TFreak. "fraggle.c",

www.phreak.org. www.phreak.org/archives/exploits/denial/fraggle.c (6 May 2003)

[16] Martin, Michael J., "Router Expert: Smurf/Fraggle Attack

Defense Using SACLS", Networking Tips and Newsletters,

www.searchnetwork.techtarget.com. Oct 2002.

http://searchnetworking.techtarget.com/tip/1,289483,sid7_gci856112,00.html (6 May 2003).

[17] TERRANCE A. ROEBUCK

http://www.crime-research.org/articles/network-security-dos-ddos-attacks

[18] Guangsen Zhang, Manish Parashar

Cooperative Mechanism Against DDoS Attacks

http://www.caip.rutgers.edu/TASSL/Papers/ddos-icics-04.pdf